STOCKS FOR BEGINNERS

Build Your Passive Income

Smart, Fast, & Effortlessly

JONATHAN S. WALKER

Copyright © 2017 Jonathan S. Walker

All rights reserved.

DEDICATION

I dedicate this book to my two beautiful children and my loving wife who have been nothing short of being my light and joy throughout the years.

Copyright 2017 by Jonathan S. Walker - All rights reserved.

The following eBook is reproduced below with the goal of providing information that is as accurate and reliable as possible. Regardless, purchasing this eBook can be seen as consent to the fact that both the publisher and the author of this book are in no way experts on the topics discussed within and that any recommendations or suggestions that are made herein are for entertainment purposes only. Professionals should be consulted as needed prior to undertaking any of the action endorsed herein.

This declaration is deemed fair and valid by both the American Bar Association and the Committee of Publishers Association and is legally binding throughout the United States.

Furthermore, the transmission, duplication or reproduction of any of the following work including specific information will be considered an illegal act irrespective of if it is done electronically or in print. This extends to creating a secondary or tertiary copy of the work or a recorded copy and is only allowed with express written consent from the Publisher. All additional right reserved.

The information in the following pages is broadly considered to be a truthful and accurate account of facts and as such any inattention, use or misuse of the information in question by the reader will render any resulting actions solely under their purview. There are no scenarios in which the publisher or the original author of this work can be in any fashion deemed liable for any hardship or damages that may befall them after undertaking information described herein.

Additionally, the information in the following pages is intended only for informational purposes and should thus be thought of as universal. As befitting its nature, it is presented without assurance regarding its prolonged validity or interim quality. Trademarks that are mentioned are done without written consent and can in no way be considered an endorsement from the trademark holder.

• • • •

CONTENTS

Part 1

Introduction

Chapter 1: What Are Penny Stocks

Chapter 2: Picking The Right Trading Strategies

Chapter 3: Getting Started With Your First Trade

Chapter 4: The Basics of Investing

Chapter 5: The Different Investing Options

Chapter 6: The Best Investment Strategies

Part 2

Chapter One: Investments With BlockChain

Chapter Two: Implementing BlockChain

Chapter Three: Smart Contacts

Chapter Four: Blockchain Pros And

Cons

Part 3

Chapter 1: Understanding Options Trading

Chapter 2: Risks And Benefits

Chapter 3: Strategies

Chapter 4: Keys To Success

Part 4

Chapter 1: 10 Popular Sources of Passive Income

Chapter 2: A Pipeline of eBooks, Apps & Blogs

Chapter 3: Real Estate Returns

Chapter 4: Investing in Stocks, Bonds & Annuities

Chapter 5: Building/Buying Websites & Domains

Chapter 6: Monitor & Adjust Your Sources

Conclusion:

• • • •

Introduction

Congratulations on purchasing your personal copy of *Stocks For Beginners: Build Your Passive Income Smart, Fast, & Effortlessly..* Thank you for doing so.

The following chapters will discuss some of the many things that you are able to do in order to grow your investment and to start making six figures in no time. The guidebook will start with some information on penny stocks, such as what penny stocks are, some of the best strategies to do well in penny stocks and how to pick the stocks that will help you to make the best decision to make money even as a beginner.

Next, we will move on to learning about some of the other investment opportunities that you can choose from t make a lot of money. We will talk about some of the basics of picking out an investment, the different types that you can pick such as bonds, the stock market, and real estate, and then some of the strategies that you can use no matter what investment you choose to go with.

When it is time to make your money grow and you want to replace your regular income, investing is the option for you. Take a look through this guidebook and learn some of the basics that you need to know about stocks, as well as some of the other investment types so that you can start making money today!

Part 1: Penny Stocks

Chapter 1: What are Penny Stocks?

Penny stocks are relatively simple, but there are a few tricks that you need to learn in order to make them work for your needs. They represent stocks that are going to have a low price, usually a price that is under a dollar, as well as a smaller market cap that is under $500 million. For the most part, when an investor is working with penny stocks, they are going to be traded off of the traditional exchanges, so you will not find them on the New York Stock Exchange or on the NASDAQ.

So why would you want to choose to work with penny stocks rather than another investment type? There are several reasons to use penny stocks, but they are often used in order to help a company procure the right capital so that the company can grow and become more powerful. Through this market, the company is able to build up the money that is needed so they can grow their business and when you pick the right company, they can make a strong investment for a low cost.

Penny stocks are going to be traded in order to benefit some of the smaller public companies. But if this company does well, and you purchased the stock over the counter before it entered the regular stock exchanges, you could get a great return on investment. Even if the company never makes it over to the regular stock exchange, many of these can still increase their profits and you can earn back on your investment.

Almost all of the penny stocks are going to be sold on over the counter exchanges. This is going to work because many of the larger exchanges are going to have stringent policies before a company can join them and trade. Most of the companies that are in penny stocks will come nowhere near reaching these stringent requirements, plus it costs a lot of money to trade on these exchanges, so it isn't possible for some smaller companies to make it work. Instead of trying to meet some of these requirements or come up with large amounts of money that they don't have, the companies are going to work with the penny stocks to get the funding they need. As the investor, you are able to capitalize on this and get some great stocks, often from some growing companies, for a low price.

As the investor, you need to remember that there will be some risk that comes with going with penny stocks. If you take the time to educate yourself and learn how to avoid some of the major mistakes that come with this investment, you are more likely to make a good income in the process, but keep in mind there are some risks and they are sometimes seen as speculative in nature, rather than as an investment.

Benefits of going with penny stocks

First, let's take some time to look at the benefits of going with penny stocks. Penny stocks could be your next big break. They are a lot of fun to work with because there are a lot of companies who are out there and are looking to use penny stocks as a way to raise capital to grow and become big. If you pick out the right company, you could be one of the first people in on it, and that stock that you got for under a dollar will end up being worth a lot of money down the road if the company does grow.

That is one of the main benefits that come with investing is that there is the potential of making a huge return on investment. You need to make sure that you purchase a stock that is at a low price, which is easy to do in penny stocks, and make sure that it has a good business plan and will survive the market, just like you would with any other investment, and you will see results. Not all companies that are in penny stocks will make it to the big leagues, but many of them can still grow and you can make money from this process.

Many investors like to go with penny stocks because they are exciting and a lot of fun to work with. It is fun and can feel great, to start out with a little bit of money and then move up and see it grow. You may not make a ton of money at first, but penny stocks can help you to start with a small investment and get it to grow. If you want to start out your portfolio and you don't have a ton of money for it, penny stocks can be a great place to start.

The negatives of penny stocks

One of the first negatives that you should be aware of when you are working in penny stocks is that many of the companies on the market are not that good. There are some companies who are really good and just need to make a few tweaks or make a bit more profit before they are able to join the regular stock markets. But many of the companies that you will find in penny stocks didn't get onto the major stock exchanges because they were just bad. You need to learn how to tell the difference between the two if you would like to make an income here.

In addition, the penny stock market is not as reliable as the major stock markets. They are unreliable and they often don't have regulations in place to determine which companies or transactions that go on with them. This doesn't mean that all of the companies are bad on the penny stock market, but since there aren't really a lot of regulations that are in place, many bad companies can sneak through, make up numbers, or hide information and it is really risky picking out the company you want to work with. You will need to be diligent and really do your research to make sure that you are picking out good companies that will earn you money over time.

Penny stocks are really interesting investments to make. They usually have stocks that come in under a dollar each, so they are a good choice for those who have limited money to invest with in the beginning. While you do need to be on guard against some of the bad companies that are able to get onto the penny stock exchange, there are still many great ones that are available that you can pick from and that will help you to make a good return on your investment!

Chapter 2: Picking the Right Trading Strategies

When it comes to working in penny stocks, or any other investment for that matter, one of the most important things that you will need to do is figure out the strategy that you want to use. The strategy is so important because it is going to determine which stocks you will purchase when you will purchase them and sell them, and what research you will do to get the results. There are many great strategies that are available and none of them are necessarily any better or worse than the others, but you will find that picking a strategy and sticking with it, rather than bouncing back and forth between a few, can make all the difference. Some of the best trading strategies that you can use when you want to trade in penny stocks include:

Scalping

This is often a popular strategy to go with because it is pretty simple to use and many beginners like this simplicity. With the idea of scalp trading, you are going to take advantage of some of the inefficiencies that are going on in the market with respect to the spread. The gap between the bid price and the asking price, which is known as the spread, can end up widening or narrowing rapidly throughout time, and even through the day and they are going to create some great selling and buying opportunities that will result in some quick profits.

To scalp, you will need to be good at watching the market and understanding the perfect time to purchase and sale. You can even look at a few markets and see if you are able to find the stocks of a company a little lower than the price of them on the other. You would then purchase the stock at the lower price before moving it over to the other market and selling it for the higher price that is demanded there. You can end up selling the stocks pretty quickly this way and while the profit may only be a little bit on each one, if you purchase quite a few stocks and do this many times, you can make a good profit.

Range trading

When things are going along as normal and all of the other things in the market are even, stocks are often going to trade inside of a set trading range each day. When you use range trading to help you to purchase and sell your penny stocks, you will try to purchase the stock when it is at the bottom of the range, and then when it gets to the top, you will want to sell it. To do this type of trading, you will want to make sure that the stocks have a consistent trading range each day so that you can make some good estimates.

So with this one, you are going to take a look at some of the history of the company, if it is available, and find out what places seem to be the high points of the stock and which ones seem to be the low points. There can be some variations of this each day, but mostly you will notice that the trend stays about the same. You will then take this information to help you make the right purchases on all of your stocks. You will be able to make a purchase of the stock when the market is at the low end of the range and then you can sell the stock when it goes back up before it goes down and you lose out again. This one will require you to spend some time looking through many graphs and charts to get the information, but it can be pretty straightforward and can make you a good profit.

Momentum trading

This is the trading option that you will go with if you are looking to go with some of the trends that are in the market to make a good profit. In basic terms, you are going to use momentum trading or trend trading to purchase a stock when it is trending up, but then you will sell the stock as soon as the trend starts to go back down. This one can be a little less risky compared to some of the others, but you have to constantly be watching the trends and the market to make sure that you get out before all of your investment is gone.

Real-time new trading.

Another option that you are able to go with when you are working on penny stocks is known as real time news trading. This is the one where you are going to have to spend some time reading or watching the news and looking for some clues as to how a market or a particular company is going to do. When you find that some good news is released, you will make the purchase, and then after that little punch up, you will sell the stock. It can also work to protect your investment because if you notice that some bad news is about to happen, you can sell the stocks without losing all the money, and then purchase them again when things settle down.

If you want to use this kind of trading strategy, you will want to make sure that you download a real-time news feed so that you are always getting information in. You also need to be able to understand what each piece of news can mean to the penny stocks that you are working with. You don't want to misunderstand what is going on and end up with selling a stock that was going up or losing out on a stock because you held onto it for too long.

When it comes to picking out the strategy that you want to use for your penny stocks, you will find that there is really no wrong answer. Each person is going to pick out a different strategy to help them out, and what works for one person is not going to work for you. Make sure to check out some of these strategies and then pick the one that works the best for you!

Chapter 3: Getting Started with Your First Trade

When you are ready to get started with your first trade in penny stocks, you will need to take a couple of steps. First, it is important to figure out the broker that you would like to work with. there are many different brokers available out there and many of them have great reputations that can help you to get done with your trading. You should compare a few of them right from the beginning, looking at the features that they offer, as well as some of the fees and costs that they will hand down to you. These will all affect how easy it is to do trades with your broker and how much you will actually make.

Once you have chosen the broker you want to work with, it is time to pick the strategy that you want to work with as well. There are many different strategies, and we discussed a few of them in the chapter above. These can all be successful based on what you would like to get out of the trading. The most important option here is to learn about the different trading strategies for penny stocks and then stick with it.

Many of the investors who end up failing are the ones who just can't seem to stick with the trading strategy that they originally picked. These are the people who will bounce back and forth between a few different options, but they never get familiar or comfortable with just one of them. You can pick any of the strategies that you would like, but you need to make sure that you are sticking with it if you want to see results.

Next on the list is to choose the stocks that you would like to invest in. This is the part that is going to take some time and you will probably need to use your chosen strategy to help you make the right decisions. When you are picking a stock to invest in, especially when it comes to the penny stock market, you want to make sure that you are being really careful. This is a fantastic market to get into, but if you are not paying attention and doing your research, you will find that your money will be all gone. Many good companies get onto the penny stock market, but so do many bad ones so you have to be diligent if you want to see success.

There are a number of things that you can do to make

sure you pick out the right stocks when working in the penny stock market. First, make sure to check out the numbers on your own. Most companies want to gain your trust and will put up their sales information and other relevant things to help you make a good decision to go with them. But since this is not always required of stocks on the penny stock market, there are some that may not provide this information at all and some that will hide factors or fudge the numbers a bit. Doing your own research, and being critical to see if that research is correct, can be a great way to ensure that you are picking out good stocks that will help you earn money.

Always be critical when it comes to picking out a stock on this market. There are too many new investors who are excited to get into the trading business and who want to be able to pick out a company that will make it big. But if you jump in too quickly and don't pay attention to what you are doing while trading, you are going to end up in trouble, and probably losing a lot of money. Make smart decisions, pick out stocks that you think will do well, and always go through and do your own research, and you are sure to see the results.

And finally, after you have chosen your strategy and the stocks that you want to invest in, you have to decide how much you want to invest. Since the penny stock market is often inexpensive, with many of the options coming in at under a dollar, it is pretty affordable for you to make some purchase and get started. But even so, you will want to set the maximum that you want to spend on the stocks, as well as how much you are willing to lose before you get out of the market. Having this plan in place ahead of time can help you to make informed decisions, rather than ones attached to your emotions, and you will see much less risk in the process.

Along the way, if you happen to have any questions about how things are working or what you should do, turning to your broker can be a great idea. They have a lot of experience working in the various investments so they should be able to answer any of the questions or the concerns that come up and they can lead you in the right direction to making a good return on your investment.

Part 2: Investors Ultimate Guide from Novice to Expert

Chapter 4: The Basics of Investing

Many people are interested in investing, but they are not sure what steps to take to get started. Many times the information that is available can be confusing and once they enter the market, it is just too much to handle. Luckily, investing doesn't have to be hard, you just need to understand how to get started. Let's take a look at some of the basics that come with investing so that you can get started.

What is investing?

first, investing is going to refer to business activities where an investor will spend money in order to gain a profit. The investment is supposed to help the investor to make money and increase the value of their money through some business activities. There are many different ways that you can do this. You can choose to start your own business and invest funds into that, you can invest in the stock market, you can choose real estate investing, and so much more. But whatever type of investment that you choose, there needs to be at least some chance of making the money back and even making a profit, otherwise, it is too risky to work with.

All of the methods above are great ways to help invest your money, you simply need to pick the one that works the best for you. You should also spend some time learning how to reduce the risk of your investment. For example, if you wanted to start a business, you would learn about the market, make a good product, and find ways to sell the product so that you can make a good profit without losing out on all of your money. If you just go into an investment without some planning, you are basically gambling rather than investing.

Before you decide to get into an investment, it is a good idea have a little bit of savings ready to go. If you make smart decisions on your investment, you shouldn't have too many issues with losing all of your money, but some investments, such as real estate, can be labor and time intensive and having some savings in hand ahead of time can reduce the risk and help reduce the stress. Then when you start to invest, make sure that a few your profits go back into your savings to help out as well.

In addition, this savings can be a great way to get started on your investment. Most of us don't have a ton of extra money lying around that we can use for this kind of investment. But if we take a few months and put a little bit back for savings, it is easier to reach our goals. Then we are able to start investing without having to cut into our income or the money that we need to pay our bills when first starting out.

Before you are able to get into a new investment you need to pick out which one you would like to go with. There ae so many different options and part of the fun is figuring out which one is the right one to match up with your skills and interest levels. If you are interested in starting your own business, you can go with that investment, but other people may be interested in working in real estate and flipping houses or renting them out. Some people want to just invest their money with a friend or family member who is starting up something, and others like to work in the different parts of the stock market. All of these have the potential of being good investments, you just need to pick one and learn how it works!

Getting started in investing is a great way to make your money work for you. There are different options and all of them are going to require you to pick out different strategies to make them work. But when you are able to do this, you can make a good income from your investment.

Chapter 5: The Different Investing Options

So, in order to be successful with investing, you need to pick out the investment opportunity that works the best for you. There are a number of options that you can pick from, but as a beginner, you will probably want to start out with just one option. Yes, there are those investors who seem to have their hands in almost every market that is out there, but this can take some time to build up and as a beginner, that is going to be way too much for you to handle. If you are still considering which type of investment you want to work with and you aren't sure where to start, check out some of these options to help make the decision easier.

The stock market

The first place that people think about when they are working on investments is the stock market. The stock market is basically a platform where shares of companies can be bought and also sold. The shares are going to be units of ownership in the company and when you purchase one of these shares, you become one of the owners of the company. Just like a traditional owner, you will be entitled to parts of the assets as well as the future profits of the company. So if the company grows and does well, you will make an income for holding onto the shares.

A common mistake with this is that new investors assume that they should purchase as many shares as they can to make a good profit. This can be one method to make a profit, but professional investors will agree that it is best to purchase stocks that have the potential to grow. You are going to make a bigger profit from 50 shares that go up to $100 each compared to 100 shares that go up to $2 each, even if you ended up purchasing them for the same total price.

There are many options when it comes to investing in the stock market. Some people choose to pick a company to invest in for the long-term and will hold onto the stock, earning a profit each quarter as long as the company does well. Day trading is popular as well and it includes you purchasing and selling the stock all on the same day to make a bunch of little profits that add up. You can also choose from forex trading, options trading, and penny stocks as well. Each of these have their own unique set of rules and own risks so make sure that you fully understand them before starting.

The bond market

Another investment type is to work with the bond market. With this option, you are taking on less risk and you know right from the beginning how much you will earn in interest, but the return on investment is lower than the stock market or other options. In the bond market, the government and other companies are looking to borrow money from investors to expand their business or to do other things to help them grow. The investor will be able to lend out this money in the form of a band, and the company or the government can then use it for their plans.

With the bond, you will invest a certain amount of money that you are not allowed to take out again until the maturity date of the bond. Sometimes this will be a few months but it can go for several years. You will get to determine the maturity date that you are comfortable with before you start. The bond will have an interest rate attached to it, which is the amount that the investor will earn on their investment when the maturity date hits. It is a safe and secure way to make a little bit of money on your investment and can help you to grow your portfolio without all the risk that is found with some of the other options.

Investing in commodities

Some investors like to invest in commodities to see a profit. Commodities are going to refer to produce that is high in demand and also publicly traded. The products themselves will not be traded on this market. The speculators and the investors in this market are going to contract for the future value of the product. Let's look at an example of coffee. Many countries will produce coffee and this can be a great commodity to work with.

With this system, you are going to pick the commodity that you want to work with and then sign a future contract for the amount that you will spend, say $100,000. If the price of the coffee goes up by the end date, you will be able to get a profit. But if for some reason the price of the coffee goes down, you will lose the money. You need to have a good idea of the market for the commodity that you want to work with and be able to estimate what is going to happen with it in the future in order to make money with this option.

Foreign exchange

Working with foreign currencies is another option that is available for a trader. With this option, you are going to make a purchase of another currency, perhaps the GBP, when the price is relatively low compared to the American one. Then you will wait until it is worth more in the future, and change it back over to the USD, making a profit in the process. For example, if you changed over to the GBP when it was worth $1.2 USD, and then held onto it for a bit until 1 GBP was worth $1.5 USD, you would make a profit of $0.30 on every dollar that you spent, which can add up if you did a larger investment.

This was traditionally a method that was only used by the banks and governments of different countries, but it is now an option that many different people are able to use thanks to the newer technology. You do need to be careful with this option though because the currency market is always fluctuating and you never know if your money is going to be worth more or less in the future. But if you are able to hold onto the money for some time and can watch the exchange rates, you can make a good profit from this option.

Starting your own business

Some people choose to start their own business in order to start a new investment. There are many options that you can choose, from brick and mortar stores to working from home. But no matter what kind of business you decide to start, you will have to put some money forward to get started. For example, even if you want to be a writer from home, you will need to invest in a good computer, some writing software, the internet, and even some storage to help keep files in order. If you want to start a clothing store, you would need to rent out a building, purchase the clothes, hire employees, and so on.

There is quite a bit of risk that can happen with starting a business, but if you think it all out, come up with a good business plan and stick with it, you can start to make a good profit from your own business. Plus, you are able to work for yourself, instead of being stuck with a boss, so it can be very appealing to many people.

The real estate market

Many people like to work with the real estate market because this is a market that is often going up. There are some different options that you are able to use when it comes to working in the real estate market, which can make this even more popular since you get to choose the one that works for you. One option that works well with real estate is flipping houses. With this option, you will purchase a home when it is really low in price, perhaps as a foreclosure or when the market is really low. Then you will make some changes to the home, fix it up and make it look nice, and then when the market starts to go up, or when the value is higher, you will sell it to make a profit.

If you are looking to get a more continuous form of income from real estate, you can choose to purchase a home and rent it out. Your rental fees should be enough to cover the cost of the home (or the mortgage) as well as the taxes, maintenance and for you to make a little bit of income. Over time, you can add in a few different properties so that you can make a full-time income in the process.

In addition, there are a lot of options that fall into the different categories. For example, working with rentals can include single family homes, duplexes, and apartment buildings and you can even work with commercial real estate as well. It all depends on the amount of work that you would like to put into the investment and how much money that you would like to earn.

As you can see, there are quite a few different options that you can pick from when it comes to working on an investment. All of these have the potential to bring you a lot of income, but you just need to pick out the one that meets your interests and that you will enjoy doing the most. Pick out your investment, and you are sure to see a great income in no time!

Chapter 6: The Best Investment Strategies

The next thing that you need to focus on, after you have been able to pick what kind of investment that you would like to work on, is to pick a good strategy that will help you to get this all going. There are a lot of investment types and all of them are going to work in a slightly different manner, so once you pick the investment option, you will need to look a bit more in depth to see what strategies are the most effective for you. But no matter what kind of investment you go with, there are a few strategies that will work for all of them including.

Buy low and sell high

In all of the investments that you work with, the goal is to purchase your asset at the lowest price that you can. If you purchase the investment at a price that is too high, you are going to lose out or not make very much money in the process. You are going to need to work on learning the market in order to understand when is the best time to make the purchase.

When it comes to the stock market, you will want to wait for the market to go down a bit, or at least a dip in the company that you are working with. This will allow you to purchase the stock at a lower price than usual, and then you just need to hold onto the stocks for a bit of time until the market goes up. Of course, you need to learn the difference between a stock being low priced because of the market and it being low priced because the company is failing.

You can use this in other investments as well. When it comes to working with real estate, you will want to look for a downturn in the housing market to get a good discount on the homes you want to purchase and then wait until the market goes back up and you can sell the home for a much higher price. The good news with real estate is that you can rent out the home, and make some income in the process, while you wait for the market to go back up.

No matter what kind of market you get into, you must make sure that you are purchasing the asset at the lowest price possible. This will ensure that your risks are lower and your profits higher. If you aren't good at reading the market and working on your strategy, you will find that you will purchase the asset at a high price and that it will be very difficult to sell it again without taking a loss. The lower that you can get the asset, without picking one that is already failing, the better off you will be when it comes to making a profit.

Be an expert in your market

The idea behind this strategy is that you stay inside just a few markets. You may look at the list of investing options above and feel that you should jump into all of them, but when you generalize in everything, you are setting yourself up for failure. As a beginner, you need to just stick with one option. This allows you to devote your time and energy to this, without becoming overwhelmed. Over time, as you become an expert in that market, you can expand out a little bit and try a few other options, but you should really just concentrate on one at a time and even when you expand, keep the markets similar.

For example, if you want to go into real estate, you should consider working first in renting out single family homes. Do that for a bit of time until you become comfortable with what you are doing and then you can consider expanding your portfolio to not only rent out these single-family homes but to also expand out to renting out duplexes and some small apartment buildings. You are still within the same field, but you are growing your income and diversifying your portfolio all at the same time.

If you are working in the stock market, you can take

kind of the same approach. You may start out with a long-term investment in a few stocks, but then over time, you may decide to add some Forex trading or some penny stocks to the mix to help diversify and make more money. You are still working in the stock market, or something similar to it though, so you can take your knowledge and expand it out to other investments.

The thing that you need to watch out for with these investments is skipping from one to another. If you have been doing real estate, you may find that it is hard to jump over to the stock market and going from the stock market to the real estate market can be tough as well, because they are really two different types of investments. Some people have been able to do it, but it is tough and you may find that it is too much to put onto your plate. It is better to just stick with the one market, become an expert in it, and then diversify within it to see the profits that you want.

Pick out financial safe havens

After you learn a bit about how to invest into the stock market or another market for investing, you may want to learn a bit about financial safe havens. These are places where you are able to transfer your money during an economic downturn and which are less likely to be negatively impacted by the market. You would put your money over to these in order to avoid losses, at least until the economy comes back around. Ideally, your safe haven is going to be able to at least beat off inflation so you will still have the same spending power later on.

There are several different types of instruments that you can use for this, but gold is one of the most popular ones. Big investors will often move their money over to gold when the economy gets tough, and this is why you will see that the price of gold will start to climb when markets like stocks and bonds start to do poorly. Gold is not the only safe haven that you can pick. In bearish markets also see a rise in treasury bills, but gold is still the most popular because the interest rates are so low on these treasury bills.

Invest actively

If you are able to get started with a larger sum of money, you are able to start investing in an active manner in the market that you choose. In order to use this particular strategy, you must learn how to become an expert in the chosen industry and focus your energy on these in order to better learn these markets and to make some of the best decisions possible to grow your money.

For example, if you are using this type of strategy, you may want to spend some time reading up on the news of any company that you are interested in investing with. In addition, you would take some time to look at the financial statements of the company, check into their management, and find out if they are growing consistently and are actually a company that you want to work with.

There are thousands of companies who are on the stock exchange and it is important that you learn how to be an active investor. Sure, you could hand over the money to a broker and hope things go well, but the most successful investors are the ones who do the research and pick out the strategy that they want to use on their own. There is nothing wrong with talking to a broker and getting some advice, but you should never let them do all of the work for you.

Focus on the goals

Before you enter into any of the investment types, you should sit down and have some clear cut goals. You want to have a purpose behind your investing and what you want to do if you are actually successful. This will help you to create a system that will lead you to meet this goal. Some people will invest in order to make some side money to help them out with bills and other things, some want to put that money towards retirement and to help them build up a little nest egg. Others are tired of working a regular job and want to be able to work for themselves. Having these goals will help you to see that success, no matter what it is.

For example, if you are looking to make this into an investment into your retirement, you may be more likely to look for long-term investment opportunities that will help you to earn a little bit over each month. If you want to make this into a full-time income, you are going to be more interested in things like flipping homes or riding some of the big waves of the stock market so you can make this income. As you can see, these are very different options of investing, but it always depends on the goals that you are trying to reach for which one you will choose.

So before you decide to go and purchase your asset or get into your chosen market, you need to sit down and decide what your goals are going to be for that investment. Then you can write down the plan that you want to follow in order to make these goals a reality. It is nice to have dreams and to hope that the investment asset that you choose will help you to get there, but if you don't plan ahead and make sure that you have the right strategy, you are never going to see the results that you want.

It is so much you are able to do when it comes to picking out an investment and seeing it grow. Picking out a good strategy will help you to really see the success that you are looking for because it leads you to pick the right asset and making decisions that will make you successful. No matter what kind of investment you choose to go with, make sure to follow some of these simple strategies and you are sure to see some of the success that you are looking for.

PART 2

Chapter One: Investments with Block Chain

The business models of several different companies in a wide range of sectors have been transformed by block chain. Looking at block chain, you are going to see that it appears to be a digital spreadsheet that is being worked on by members inside of an organization. The "digital spreadsheet" is going to be on a decentralized network.

Due to the way that block chain is written, it has some unique factors that are not going to be able to be understood, even by the investors that think that they can make a profit on that technology. Block chain is not like traditional trading because it has several different levels that are used.

Block chain offers at least five different ways that you can make an investment that will benefit you later on.

   1. Stockpile coins

Many investors are stockpiling gold so that they can

wait to sell it whenever the price goes up sometime in the future. However, there are other investors that are stockpiling bitcoins. Stockpiling gold and stockpiling bitcoins are going to each have their advantages as well as their disadvantages but what it comes down to is the supply and demand. Whenever the supply is limited, the demand is going to go up, therefore, the value is going to increase which is going to be the opportune time to sell what it is that they are stockpiling.

2. Penny stocks

Penny stocks are a cryptocurrency like bitcoins just like Ether is a cryptocurrency, but they all work on a different system due to the fact that they are competing with bitcoin.

3. Crowdfunding with altcoin

Crowdfunding is a method that you can use whenever you are trying to raise capital for an investment. The coins are not going to need to be used when you are dealing with crowdfunding. Instead, people are going to give you coins before you start mining which is typically done before a system is opened to the public.

4. Angel funding and start up ventures

Block chain makes it possible for a great number of entrepreneurs and investors to come together and find each other to get funding.

5. Pure block chain technology

The technology behind block chain is on the rise, and the companies that are taking advantage of it are getting their name out there so that they can be better known whenever you find the block chain technology everywhere. A company by the name of Global Arena Holdings uses the block chain technology as leverage in getting their votes verified.

Chapter Two: Implementing Block Chain

Knowing how you want to use block chain is vital before you get too deep into it. Block chain offers two ways to use their system, but ensure that you are choosing the one that is best for you. Typically people use block chain with an individual account.

With an individual account, you need to set up your wallet. Your wallet is going to be where you keep all of your bitcoins and will run off of most mobile devices and computers. Digital wallets are more secure than real wallets because they are not going to be stolen and they are most likely not going to be hacked.

When you use a software wallet, you are not going to be required to have a third party service for the wallet to be downloaded. Once it has been placed on your computer, you are going to have all of your transactions at your fingertips.

Next, you need to acquire bitcoins. You have the option to trade bitcoins for goods or services that you may be able to offer to those in the bitcoin system; however, it is hard to find someone who is willing to trade bitcoins because they do not want to give up their coins. You can also buy bitcoins in the marketplace where you can spend real world money and purchase as many coins as you want.

Lastly, you have the option to mine coins. Programs can be placed on your computer that will use a CPU that is customized to assist you in making a quick profit without you having to do many of anything.

You should make sure that your wallet is secured! Encrypt your wallet so that you are not leaving it open to hackers who want to steal your coins. If your coins are stolen, or bitcoin does not offer you an option where they will replace them because they are your responsibility.

Bitcoins can be spent just like regular money can be.

However, you need to find a merchant who will accept bitcoins as payment.

Chapter Three: Smart Contracts

Smart contracts are probably going to be the aspect of block chain that will most likely be championed in the future. A smart contract is just a type of computer code that is activated once the block chain as a whole register that a predetermined incident has occurred. The smart contract is then given its own block and distributed as part of the chain.

While it may seem complicated, you can think of them in much the same way certain functions in a checking account work. In most checking accounts, automated deductions can be set up either by the user or by a third party with the user's permission. A smart contract works in broadly the same way but from a decentralized—not centralized--position. Put another way; a smart contract is the computer code equivalent of the legalese in a contract that stipulates how and when all the little details are carried out.

Additionally, as long as the smart contract is

generated on a public block chain, then, unlike in the banking example, there is no third party (such as the bank) who is able to step in and actively prevent the transaction from occurring. The transaction is equally secure if it is performed by a bank or by a block chain. This is due to the extreme type of security that is built into the block chain model, the fact that the data is decentralized, and the extreme cost required to hijack a block chain.

What's more, unlike with traditional contracts, smart contracts that are executed via block chain are completely public and viewable by anyone with a copy of the chain. This means that the smart contract is never open for debate or discussion; it is purely an expression of the facts as they are truly stated. This can be seen as a miracle or a curse, of course, depending on the nature of the information being made public.

A smart contract is where a computer protocol can

facilitate, verify, and even enforce the negotiation and performance of a contract in which the contractual clause becomes unnecessary.

The smart contract can also have a user interface that will emulate the logic of a contractual clause(s). The proponents of a smart contract claim that many different kinds of the contractual clauses may thus be made partial or even fully self-executing, self-enforcing, or possibly even both.

Smart contracts are going to aim to provide the security that is superior to any traditional law contract. This will, therefore, reduce the transaction costs that are associated with the process of drawing up a contract.

Common usage cases

With the rising market penetration of various financial technologies, smart contracts are becoming more and more prevalent. A big reason for that is because they are simplifying many common contract usage cases.

For example, they are already making it easier for users to update various contract terms in real time, despite it taking days for physical copies to move back and forth to perform the same function. This not only improves the speed with which such processes can be performed but also greatly increases the odds of their accuracy remaining at acceptable levels throughout.

Smart contracts also activate automatically once certain real world conditions have been met, which means they require fewer resources to be utilized to the fullest. While this won't mean much to most users who use them infrequently, for business to business transactions, the savings will likely be substantial. The guaranteed and secure nature of a smart contract also means that it can be executed upon without the need for a third party to guarantee the transaction via escrow, reducing the closing costs of the contract on all sides.

Financial institutions will also find smart contracts

useful in numerous ways. In regard to trade clearing or settlement scenarios, the final results relating to settlements, transfers, and trades is tallied automatically. Smart contracts can also be used when it comes to coupon payments, specifically to return principal on expired bonds. They also work with insurance claims as a means of minimizing errors and streamlining the flow of work between departments. Finally, they are also known to improve the regulation of Internet of Things services.

In the health care sector, smart contracts are known to offer up numerous advantages. For instance, they improve the accuracy with which medical records are updated as patients are transferred between departments. They can also be used to monitor the health of the population as a whole via public blockchains that update automatically and pay participants for using their information. Smart contracts are also already in use in many Internet of

Things devices where they are used to determine the success of fitness goals and release rewards accordingly.

In the music industry, smart contracts are already being put to work tracking royalties for song usage and distributing payments accordingly. It is also being put to work on a smaller scale to enhance person to person interactions and is predicted to lead to things like trading energy credits and increased peer lending opportunities. This same technology is currently being adapted for use with the Tesla electric car, whereby users can charge at any charging station and be billed for the transaction automatically.

It is also changing the way large products are shipped and tracked by sending out automated documentation as various production pieces make their way through processing, and on to shipping. This can even be cued to the input of certain signatures, meaning the process is seamless for signing the contract to receiving the goods. Later on down the line, if there are questions about the quality of the shipment, then the entire route the product took from creation to delivery can be tracked. This is due to the fact that it is on the same block chain that enables the creation of the contract in the first place.

For credit enforcement, the smart contracts are becoming an extension of property law. The credit agreements are going to disable the product that you have purchased if you fail to make the payments that you agreed to make. For example, if you buy a new car on credit and fail to make your payment. Then the doors to your car are going to lock and then drive itself back to the showroom.

However, most electrical products come with what is known as a kill switch that can be disabled should a condition not be met between the two parties. This would happen if the payments were being made through a public channel such as cryptocurrency.

Chapter Four: Block Chain Pros and Cons

Block chain is not immune to have its pros and cons just like everything else that you can get involved in. While block chain is versatile, there are still those who are hesitant to switch over to the new technology when they can just stick to the methods they know work.

Block chain will protect your identity as well as work with you to make sure that your money is not stolen. Your personal information does not have to be entered into the block chain system in order for any transactions to be completed. It is going to be much like when you buy something with cash. You do not even have to enter a real email address. The block chain system gives you an email address, so that will change each time that you make a transaction on the system.

If there is any cost to send or receive a payment on

the block chain system, it is not going to be a large fee. Any payments that go international will not force you to pay things such as transaction or exchange fees that a traditional financial institute would force you to do. Therefore, this will help keep all of your fees down when you find yourself traveling abroad.

One of the biggest cons that you are going to find with block chain is that you do not have the ability to reverse a transaction once you have made it. So, you need to be cautious when you are sending out coins because once it has been spent, there is a possibility that you are not going to get a refund from that person. Basically, keep a good handle on where you send your coins and have extra security on your system so that your coins cannot be stolen by a hacker.

Keeping your bitcoins means that you are going to have to deal with volatility. The value of bitcoins fluctuates with time and the longer you hold onto them, the less value they are going to hold when you are ready to spend them. So, you are going to be gambling with your coins and their value the longer that you hold onto them.

There are several companies such as Etsy and TigerDirect that are going to accept bitcoins as a form of payment rather than taking cash. However, big companies like Walmart and Target have not gotten on board yet, and there is no telling when they are going to get on board with bitcoin considering how well they are doing as it is. But, it is very likely that they are going to look into accepting bitcoins as the value of bitcoins goes up making it to where more and more people are using it.

Rather than being like a credit card, bitcoins are like cash. There are no extensions in the warranty that you have to deal with, but then again you are not going to have the rewards that you can get when it comes to using a credit card. Some places do not allow you to use a credit card for whatever policy reason that they have so then you are always going to worry about that as well. Then there are the fees and the added headache of if you do not pay it, it is going to affect your credit score.

Cash, on the other hand, is taken everywhere, there are no fees, in fact, there are many times that you end up getting a discount because you used cash. With bitcoin, you are going to be able to use it without the headache of late fees or other things that you are going to have to worry about with a credit card.

The biggest similarity that bitcoins has with credit cards is the fact that it is not going to be accepted everywhere.

On the business side of it, using bitcoin is going to save you money. If you are going to use services such as Coinbase, then the first million dollars that you make by accepting bitcoins is going to be free for you. It is from here that you are going to begin to pay at least one percent on all of the transactions that you do. However, this is still going to be considerably less than what you are paying in order to accept credit cards.

Exchanges that are doing with bitcoins can be converted easily without the need to worry about risking a lot of volatility. Not to mention, bitcoin eases any worries that you are going to have of chargebacks or even hackers getting into your system and stealing your customer's credit card numbers. The merchants that use bitcoin are normally going to work off of a tablet or even a smartphone when they are accepting a payment. This is an added benefit because you will not need a big fancy system that can only stay in one place. Therefore, you are going to be able to take your business with you anywhere and accept payments. Which is a major plus for your business!

PART 3

CHAPTER 1: UNDERSTANDING OPTIONS TRADING

Options trading, also known as *binary options trading,* is just like forex and stock trading. However, you do not need to buy currencies or stocks. Instead, you simply predict whether the value of an underlying asset will increase or decrease at a specified time. It is this simplicity of options trading that attract so many investors. It is an option contract that has a fixed payout.

Options trading vs. forex and stock trading

In forex and stocking trading, you buy currencies or stocks and sell them for profit. In options trading, you do not need to buy any trading asset. You only predict whether the price of an underlying asset will be higher or lower than its current price at the expiration date. Also, in forex and stock trading, your profit will depend on the increase in the value of a particular currency or stock that you have purchased. In options trading, the potential profit is fixed and is revealed to you even before you commence a trade.

It is not uncommon for forex and stock traders to wait for weeks and months just to see a little profit from their investment. Many times, they even lose their investment without any chance of getting any profit. This happens when the price of their stocks or currency drops. With options trading, there is always a potential to earn a big amount of profit even when the price of an underlying asset decreases. You do not have to wait for weeks or months; you can double, or even triple, your investment in a few minutes.

Options trading vs. gambling

There are similarities between options trading and gambling. In some jurisdictions, options trading is literally considered gambling. Just like the casino game called *baccarat* where you decide whether the winning hand is *banker* or *player*, in options trading, you will decide whether the value of an underlying asset will rise (Call) or fall (Put) at the expiration time. Just like the table games in the casino, there is a fixed payout for a favorable outcome.

You might be wondering, "Is options trading gambling?" It depends. If you do options trading by relying on guesswork and pure luck, then you are gambling. However, if you consider every wager that you make an investment decision and take the serious effort to study the market and research the different underlying assets being traded, then you are an investor or trader.

It does not really matter whether you see yourself as a gambler or a trader. In the end, what matters is how much profit you have made, if any.

The Basics

Let us move on to the specific parts of options trading. Do not worry; options trading is very easy. You can learn the basics in less than five minutes. It is only like speculating the outcome of a coin flip.

Call vs. Put

There are only two main options to choose from. In options trading, you just have to know whether the outcome will be a *Call* or a *Put*. Simple, right?

Choose the Call option if you predict that the price of an underlying asset will be *above* its current price at the expiration date.

Choose the Put option if you predict that the price of an underlying asset will be *below* its current price at the expiration date.

These two terms are referred to by many names, depending on the trading platform that you use. They are also known as Up/Down, Above/Below, Rise/Fall, and others.

Strike price

This refers to the price at which an asset can be bought or sold at a certain time. In options trading, this simply refers to the Call or Put option. The Call option is the value at which the underlying asset can be bought, while the Put option is when it can be sold at a specified time.

Expiration time

The expiration time, or simply expiry time, signifies

the end of a trading period. This is also the time when you can determine whether or not you have made the right investment decision. Therefore, this is the moment when you will experience a profit or a loss.

In-the-money vs. out-the-money

In-the-money is a *win*. It means that you have made the right investment decision and earned a profit. On the contrary, out-the-money means that you have lost your wager.

Long-term option

In options trading, you get to choose how long a trade will last (expiration date). A long-term option simply refers to a trade that is long as 24 hours or more. A long-term option can last for a day, weeks, and months.

Speed option

As the name already implies, speed options are trades that last for a short period of time. This can be as fast as 30 seconds, a minute, or up to five to fifteen minutes, depending on the platform that you use.

Assets

Assets are valuable financial instruments. In options trading, you do not have to purchase any asset, you just have to determine if the value of an asset will be greater than or lower than its current price at the expiration time.

When trading binary options, the following assets are traded:

- stocks
- index

- commodities
- currency pairs

Bear market vs. bull market

On the one hand, a bear market means that the prices of certain assets are decreasing or are about to decrease. On the other hand, a bull market means that the prices of certain assets are increasing or are about to increase.

Take note, however, that even though a bear market is considered a negative sentiment, it does not affect you as a trader. In fact, you can even profit from it. This is because options trading has a dual nature: You can make a good amount of profit whether the price of certain underlying assets increase or decrease, provided you choose the right option (Call vs. Put).

Brokers and trading platforms

Before you can start trading binary options, you need to open an account with a broker. You can find many brokers when you make a search online. However, you need to choose a broker that will best suite your needs. Unfortunately, there are also scammers out there, so it is best to work only with a broker that has a well-established reputation.

Here is a list of trusted brokers. Take note that trading platforms may change their policies and management team. Therefore, even the most trusted brokers may no longer be a good choice tomorrow. Before you open an account, check the latest ratings and reviews given by other traders.

- iq option (www.iqoption.com)
- OptionRobot (www.optionrobot.com)
- Automated Binary (www.automatedbinary.com)
- Finpari (www.finpari.com)

- 24option (www.24option.com)
- fortuneJack (www.fortunejack.com) *bitcoin casino with binary options*

Important note:

Be sure to check the *banking options*. Many brokers accept many methods to make a deposit but only have limited options for making a withdrawal.

CHAPTER 2: RISKS & BENEFITS

Like any business venture, there are a number of risks and benefits associated with options trading. Here are the things that you can expect:

Market risk

The market is composed of real people. This is why it is extremely volatile. And, although there are methods that have been developed to predict market movements, there is no guaranteed way to determine how the market responds.

Lack of ownership

In options trading, you only wager on the future valuation of an underlying asset. Therefore, you do not exercise any right of ownership over any stock or asset.

High-risk investment

Like any other business that offers a high reward, the risk involved is also high. Unlike in trading stocks where you get to keep a losing stock with an opportunity that its price will soon increase or at least sell the stock to cut down your losses, you do not get to keep anything if you encounter a loss in options trading. In options trading, when you lose a trade, you lose the whole amount that you wager on that particular trade.

Limited opportunity

In options trading, the potential payout is already fixed even before you commence a trade. You cannot get a profit higher than the fixed payout. In forex or stock trading, the potential profit is almost limitless.

No liquidity

There is no liquidity because you do not have ownership of the stock or asset being traded. When you commence a trade, you just have to wait for the trading period to end and hope for the best. However, liquidity should not be an issue. After all, there are trades that can last for just a day, even less.

Losing is normal

Although there are people who rake in serious profits with options trading, the majority of traders lose their money, and they lose it within a short period of time.

If your entrepreneurial spirit remains strong and convinced despite the risks that you will encounter along your journey, then it is time for you to know the notable benefits of options trading.

The Benefits

High Return

For those who engage in forex or stock trading, a 50% is already considered high. And, usually, they would have to wait for months just to get a 50% profit. Most of the time, they do not even reach 50%. With options trading, getting a 90% per trade is normal. You can double your money in less than an hour.

Simplicity

It is the beautiful simplicity of options trading that makes it very attractive. You do not need to have any trading portfolio or any gambling experience. You can learn and start earning money with options trading almost instantly.

Fixed payout

Unlike other investment opportunities where you do not know how much money you can make, options trading lets you know the exact amount that you can profit before you commence a trade.

Quick turnover rate

Options trading allows you to choose just how long you want a trade to last. With speed trading, you can make multiple trades in less than five minutes.

Asset variety

Since you do not have to purchase any asset or currency, you have all the available underlying assets to choose from. Also, the minimum amount per trade is usually low, so you can easily diversify the assets that you invest in.

Controlled risk

You do not have to worry about hidden charges or

surcharges. Whatever amount that you spend for a particular trade is your total risk. If you just want to risk $100, then simply invest $100, and there is nothing else that you should worry about.

Instant trading

Most established brokers offer a mobile phone feature. This will allow you to manage your account and commence a trade anytime and anywhere.

CHAPTER 3: STRATEGIES

Most people who lose their money with options trading either have no strategy at all and just rely on pure luck, or have a poor and underdeveloped strategy. If you want to rake in serious profits with options trading, you need to have a solid strategy. Unlike casino games where you simply have to vary the amount of your bets, success in options trading requires serious research, analysis, and practice.

Fundamental analysis

Fundamental analysis is considered the lifeblood of investment. This is the key to increasing your chances of making a profit. Remember that the market is run by real people and businesses, In fundamental analysis, you need to gather various information and analyze the economy, financial statements of businesses, as well as the latest news, among others. By analyzing these data, you can come up with a better investment decision. For example, if there is a report that the problem of the high unemployment rate has just been resolved in the U.S., and all other things being normal, then you can expect the value of the U.S. currency to increase.

If you like numbers, then fundamental analysis is the way to go. However, it is not recommended for speed options. This is because economic and business changes take time. It is best to use this method for trades that last for more than 12 hours.

Technical analysis

If you do not like analyzing lots of numbers, then technical analysis may be for you. Technical analysis is more visual. You will be analyzing charts and graphs. Technical analysis is excellent for fast trading or speed options. The proper way to use this method is to view the available graphs and look for patterns.

A note about patterns: Patterns depend on the latest trend. Is it a bull or a bear market? The risk here is that trends are not permanent. They change —and they usually change quickly. The key here is to find a pattern and be able to place your wager just before the trend changes.

Algorithmic and signals

By using computer programs and apps that can be installed on your computer, you will know where to invest in. This is an easy and quick way to come up with a decision; however, this method is not recommended because it is unreliable. There is simply no computer program that can accurately read the market's movement. However, this can be useful as secondary information.

Co-integration trading

This strategy uses the correlation that is created between two underlying assets. This usually occurs when two assets are in the same industry or have the same market. Due to their high correlation, you will notice that their prices are always close to each other. Hence, when a sudden significant gap appears between their prices, there is the highest probability that their prices will soon be close to each other again. So, you either place a Call option on the stock whose value has dropped or a Put option on the stock with a higher price.

Aggressive betting

As the name already implies, it is aggressive when you

wager a big percentage of your total investment per trade, like wagering 20% per trade. Of course, the most aggressive way is to wager your whole investment on a single trade, but such is not recommended.

A famous aggressive betting strategy that is widely used by gamblers is known as the Martingale. This is where you double your wager after every loss. For example, first, you wager $10. If you lose the trade, you then wager $20. If you lose the trade again, you next wager $40, and so on... until you win a trade. When you win a trade, you go back to your initial wager of $10.

Although the Martingale looks feasible and reasonable, it is not effective in the long run. Unfortunately, it is not surprising to experience a series of wrong investment decisions. If you get really unlucky, you may even make 10 wrong decisions in a row. There only use this strategy for a short term, and be sure to back it up with sufficient research.

Conservative betting

Your betting strategy is considered conservative if you only use a small percentage of your total investment per trade, preferably just around 1%-3%. This is good if you already have a well-developed strategy that has a high rate of success.

Corrective

This is a good strategy to use when you see a sudden and significant increase or decrease in price, especially when such price spike is not clearly justified by existing factors. In such a case, you can expect for the price to balance out by reverting to its original value prior to the price spike, or somewhat close to it.

Breakout

This strategy works well with currency pairs. When a currency pair follows a tight or close price difference, and if you see them break out, the probability is high that their prices will continue to breakout. Although they will most likely revert to their normal price range, such will take time.

Asset mastery

Pick any underlying asset of your choice. Now, find out everything that you can about your chosen asset. Follow on the news and gather as much data as you can about that asset. Do this on a regular basis, preferably daily. You will notice that the more you know about a particular asset, the better predictions you can make. This also confirms that the market does not move at random.

CHAPTER 4: KEYS TO SUCCESS

Regardless whether you only want to trade for profit or for fun, you should know the best practices that can help increase your chances of success and minimize your losses.

Money management

No matter how well developed your strategy is or how much you have increased your success rate, you can lose your investment if you fail to manage your money properly. Also, do not use the money that you need to cover your household bills and other obligations. Do not forget that options trading is a high-risk investment.

Cash out

An important part of money management is learning

to cash out. Unfortunately, many traders do not cash out their profits. Although it is good to grow your funds, you should still cash out from time to time. Take note that your profits only become real when you turn them into real cash; otherwise, they are nothing but numbers on a screen and almost have no difference with demo credits. Therefore, always cash out, you do not have to cash out everything, if you want, you can just cash out 20% of your profits on a regular basis.

Research and analysis

The possibility of doing a research and analysis is what separates options trading from gambling. You need to research and be updated on the news about the businesses themselves, as well as the factors that affect business performance. When analyzing, you need to drop your personal preferences and see everything as they are. Your investment decision must be based on facts without any bias. Research is key. Remember that the outcome of every trade and the movements of the graphs are mere reflections of reality. The more you know about the economy, real people, and real businesses, the better you can make an investment decision.

Focus on the assets

Although the graphs and charts may reveal to you certain patterns, it is worth noting that such patterns are not always present. And, many times, they do not stay for so long. After all, trends are meant to change, considering that the market is alive and continues to move. When making an investment decision, be sure that you have good information on the asset that is the subject of your trade. It must be emphasized that the more you know about a particular asset, the higher is the probability of making the right investment decision.

The importance of keeping a journal

Although having a journal is not a requirement, writing a trading journal can be very helpful. You do not need to be a professional writer; you only need to be open and honest when you write your journal.

A journal will allow you to think outside the box and be a better trader. You can write anything in your journal. You can write about your new learnings, mistakes, or any adjustments that you make to your strategy. Should you decide to use a journal, be sure to update it regularly

Start small

It can be very tempting to invest a lot in a particular trade when you know that you have researched a great deal just to make that trade. However, if you are a beginner, it is best to start small and focus on increasing your success rate. First, you need to get a feel of options trading and develop your strategy. If it is your first time to trade, do not focus on making money right away. After all, once you have enough experience and confidence, you can easily increase the amount that you invest per trade. To have a good and steady profit, aim to have a success rate of at least 60%-70%.

Focus on the numbers

There are ways to somehow manipulate the stocks for a short period of time. Especially these days when you can easily and quickly send a message to the world with just a few clicks of a mouse, some people are able to make their stocks look more attractive than they really are. Unfortunately, even the media may have its own preferences and prejudices. And many so-called "experts" on options trading cannot be trusted. Therefore, you need to focus on the numbers. Words are easy to manipulate and misinterpret, but numbers do not lie. When numbers are unduly manipulated, such fraudulent scheme tends to be obvious.

Do not chase after your losses

When you engage in options trading, you should be prepared to encounter some losses. You cannot expect to make the right investment decisions all the time.

Losses are part of this kind of investment. The important thing is that the outcome of all your trades results in a positive profit.

Never chase after your losses. If you do, there is a higher risk of losing more money. Instead, be positive and focus on your profits, and how to profit some more.

Most people chase after their losses by increasing the amount of their wager per trade. This is risky because your strategy may not be suited for an aggressive betting, and your funds may not be enough to handle such big wagers.

Develop your strategy

In options trading, developing a strategy simply does not end. This is because you are dealing with a living and continuously evolving market. Therefore, you should continuously work on your strategy. It must be flexible enough to adapt to market changes and effective enough to make a decent amount of profit.

Have your own understanding of the market

True experts do not have the same strategy or share the same viewpoints all the time. They are experts because they have developed their own understanding of the market, and they can justify their views no matter how odd they may be. In the same manner, you also need to develop your own understanding of options trading and the market. In the beginning, you can rely on expert tips and advice, but soon you need to have your own way of making an investment decision. After all, nobody can get rich just by relying on expert advice. Also, out of the many people out there who claim to be "experts," only a few of them are true experts. Most of these "experts" have more losses than profits.

Practice

The only way to truly learn options trading is by actual practice. It is experience that will make you a real binary options trader. Take note that practicing does not only mean making a series of trades. In options trading, placing a trade is the easiest part. True practice means doing research and studying the various underlying assets, businesses, as well as the market behavior, among others.

PART 4

What Can Passive Income Do for You?

We've already determined your passive income is going to work for your "future" financial freedom, so it's necessary not to expect instant gratification, right? Wrong! Once you begin seeing the results of your passive income streams working on your behalf, you'll feel gratified seeing your money multiply. What you'll learn are ways to manage and control your future that you never thought yourself capable of doing. One success will build upon another until your confidence, and increased feelings of self-worth will be almost as rewarding as the additional income you are generating. Here are some of the things you can expect when you have created several successful streams of passive income.

- You have the freedom to work on what you feel passionate about rather than being trapped by a 9-5 job with limited monetary gain and even less personal gratification.
- You can plan to retire early, explore magnificent world class destinations that you may never have

had the opportunity to do without your passive income.

- You can spend more time with your family and not continue to be a slave to your job.
- You can help others and volunteer for heartfelt causes.
- You can live a healthier, stress-free life.
- You can let your imagination and creative spirit run wild—writing the next best seller, painting on the beach, or exploring faraway lands and people.
- Bottom line—you can live the life of those you currently envy!

Sounds Good—But Where Do You Start?

I would love to say that you have already started by reading this book, but I'd be remiss if I didn't explain a sad fact. Many people read about creating passive income, and that is all the further they get to achieving it. Either they think they don't have the skills or knowledge, or they lack the motivation to do what it takes today to plan for a better tomorrow. Don't be one of those people. Every new endeavor comes with an initial energy and inner spark that excites and inspires you. Unfortunately, if that initial spark isn't attended to, it will not grow into a raging fire that spurs you to continue to work all the avenues of passive income that could create financial freedom. The enthusiasm you may be feeling as you read these pages needs to be protected and nurtured—worked into a viable fuel that speeds your progress. It's not only important to know how to start, but you must know how to push yourself through some of the more demanding up-front challenges of creating passive income. You must be "active" in your pursuit of "passive" income.

Here are three tips to help you get a good start in building a stream of passive income.

1. Ask yourself why you want to do this? Are you only in it for the money, or would you like to do something for which you feel passion? Very important question. Many of the streams of passive income you will be interested in pursuing will require passionately presenting your ideas to others. People can spot a "huckster' a mile away, so whatever you choose to do, make it something you believe in and enjoy. Don't just make it an idea or product you need to push off on people to make money.

2. If you don't have much money to invest in the beginning, that's okay. However, count on spending a good deal of time in planning and preparing to take your product or service to market and make it a success. Take the time to consider your consumer, to understand their needs and wants so that you make sure your choice will be beneficial and long-lasting. If you

are working a full-time job while you're getting your passive income going, know that you may not have a lot of time to be a Sunday afternoon couch potato anymore.

3. Realize that there is no such thing as passive income that is 100% passive, no matter how much planning and preparation you have given it. Even investments in stocks require you to check on the market and frequently buy and sell to optimize your investment. If you've chosen eBooks, blogs, websites, or apps, you still need to continue to produce, so you have a pipeline of possibilities. Though maintenance may be minimal as your passive income matures, you'll still want to devote time to new endeavors. If you are passionate about what you are doing, you'll enjoy the process as much as the end results (1).

Some passive income streams require a substantial amount of money to start. If those are the types of passive income that flip your switch, you'll need to save some money first. For example, if real estate or stocks are what interests you, then you have two way to begin. Either you win the lottery or inherit, or you do it the old-fashioned way and save. Instead of having a Christmas or vacation fund, you may want to start a passive income fund. Save a little out of your check each month and sock it away. Consider cleaning out your garage and having a large yard sale. Take the proceeds from the sale, and begin investing just a little to get your feet wet. Once you experience some success, you can take your profit and reinvest, building and diversify your investments.

That word "diversify" is crucial when it comes to planning what type of passive incomes to choose. There is wisdom in the adage, "Don't put all your eggs in one basket." If you have several different things working for you, when demand is down for one, it may be up for another. Plus, who wants to do the same thing over and over, when you could be enjoying exploring different things every day? Leave that for your 9-5 job. Speaking of which, the earlier you can begin building an ongoing stream of passive income, the better. Waiting until you retire to decide whether you'll have enough money to retire comfortably, is like leaving your car windows rolled down in a rain storm and worrying if your seats will get wet. Of course, they will!

Sure, if you're retired, you'll have all the time in the world to invest in building passive income—but, no money. Even the smallest of ventures usually requires some monetary investment. Waiting until you're older to think about your future is never a good idea.

So, where and when do you start? There's no time like right now. Here are five easy steps to get started on building a steady stream of passive income.

Step #1:

Make a list of things you love to do. Include hobbies, unique talents you possess, creative outlets you have, or perhaps objects you have collected over the years.

Step #2:

Write down what you feel would be a comfortable and believable amount of money for you to make in a year's time with your stream of passive income.

Step #3:

Now compare the two steps, looking at what you could do that would contribute to your goal. For example: If your goal was to make $10,000 per year in passive income, what's on that list in step #1 to help you do that? Is there anything that would appeal to a significant number of people if you were to market that product or service? Let's say your hobby was to play the piano. Could you write an eBook on how to play the piano? Could you have an online course, teaching beginners how to play? Could you have YouTube lessons that would complement your book, demonstrating a step-by-step course? Could you have a website offering several beginner books or beginner sheet music for sale that would best help the beginner? Could you hold a webinar to teach several enrollees to play at once, charging a reasonable fee, of course?

Once you've given full reign to your imagination, the list of possible products and services are endless. The key is to let your mind run with wild abandon to all the possibilities. Make sure you write them all down, no matter how silly they might sound. Somewhere inside the silliness might just be an amazing way to earn passive income.

Step #4:

Start small. If you need inventory for your passive income, don't buy a warehouse full and then pay to have it stored—test the waters. In case this particular type of passive income was not successful, you don't want to lose too much on a fail. There will be some things in which you invest time and money, which go anywhere. Don't get discouraged. All it could mean is that you need to do a better job of planning and preparing before investing the time and money.

Step #5:

Involve a well-wisher. What I mean by this is, solicit the support of someone who cares about your success. If it's a close family member, make sure they will benefit from the sacrifices they will be asked to make as well. For instance, if you are investing your previously free time or some of your family time to work on your own ventures, then an involved spouse will be less likely to burden you with complaints. Share your goals and get that person aboard right from the get go so their participation can help minimize your time investment.

Most importantly, believe in pursuing passive. If you have things on your list that you like but don't believe anybody else would, it's probably not going to be an excellent addition to your stream of passive income. It might be better to postpone that one until you have some successes under your belt. Early success is excellent inspiration for continued activity. Even though your ideas may be out of the norm, that's the great thing about passive income. Nothing's off limits. If your idea sounds too far out there, find an expert that you respect in the field of your interest, and let that expert help you get grounded. Who knows, with just a little help your idea could go from far out to far-reaching, attracting others to your cause or venture.

With expectations intact, now give all these things some thought and continue reading to see some specifics on how to make your passive income prosperous.

CHAPTER 1: 10 POPULAR SOURCES OF PASSIVE INCOME

Almost anything can become a source of passive income, so what you choose to include in your stream should be what excites you—what you feel passionate about so that you can enjoy the journey of building a financially free future. Learn to think about passive income differently. It's not a job, not an obligation or responsibility; it's more like a fun hobby that happens to earn you money. The more you enjoy working on building a passive income, the more you'll succeed at creating something special that will attract consumers.

Although we are going to suggest ten sources that others have found to be profitable and exciting, your sources of passive income are only limited by the bounds of your creativity. This chapter will introduce you to some tried and proven streams of passive income. In the chapters to follow, we will go into depth on how to begin building each one of these sources. The exciting thing about passive income is that you get to take a source, explore and expand all the possibilities of turning that source into a stream of revenue, and discover how you can motivate and inspire others to join in, participating in the adventure because they believe in you and your offering.

The following ten sources of passive income have helped many beginners build their financial futures, but it does come at a cost. Typically, the more money you invest, the less time it requires to maintain the stream. However, many of the suggested sources don't require a great deal of monetary investment, so don't think you must have a sizeable nest egg before starting your stream of passive income. Be prepared, though, to spend your spare time away from the television and into ways you can generate avenues of income.

10 Sources of Passive Income

1. Writing eBooks

You don't have to be an excellent writer to build a pipeline of eBooks that will earn you money while you move forward with other sources. All you need to do is find topics you know enough about to help or interest others. The great subject matter is key to success in eBooks. Once you have established topics you think readers would enjoy and benefit from; you're halfway there. We'll show you how to start a pipeline of eBooks without ever writing a word.

2. Developing Apps

Again, you don't have to be an expert programmer to design and develop an incredible app that would be useful to others. As we go, we'll show you how you can hire the work done efficiently and competently, and get onto making money. We'll teach you how to identify a problem and create a solution with your app.

You'll learn how to design and market your app so that users will be eager to see what's coming next. It won't just stop with one app. Once you learn the process, you'll begin to think like a real problem solver. Soon, you'll be an expert at discovering and designing apps that help people in their day-to-day lives. Creating passive income through the development of apps can be a rewarding endeavor—both financially and emotionally!

3. Creating Blogs

When you are building your sources of passive income, you'll want to do so with things in which you are already familiar. Don't worry if you are not yet an expert, once you've completed your research and discovery, you can tap into all the experts' information and learn to organize it in a way that is unique, interesting, and easy for consumers to follow. Highly intelligent people are not experts at everything, they simply know how to surround themselves with other very smart individuals who are experts, and then they tap into that expert knowledge and skill to build their own success.

Blogs are a way to create a following where readers recognize the value of the information you impart. Think of blogs as a vehicle in which to deliver information and inspire people to continue to learn more about the topic you have chosen. You're the teacher, gathering eager students whose goal is to absorb all your knowledge and skills and apply your expertise.

4. Developing Websites

Again, don't worry about not knowing how to write code or develop a website. You just need to be the idea person. Yours is to create and inspire; let others who are expert web developers activate your ideas. We'll show you in a later chapter all the amazing things you can do with a website that works while you're not.

5. Investing in Stocks

    Some people think they must have a lot of money and knowledge to invest in stocks. That's a myth. Remember what I said about starting small and then letting your investments work for you. When you invest a little, chances are you're not going to make an overnight killing on a magical rise in your stock's value. You'll invest a little, and you'll make a little, and then you'll reinvest a little more until you build up that nest egg. Keep your energy invested in the journey, and for the moment, don't worry about the end destination.

6. Investing in Bonds

    Investing in bonds is a long-term endeavor. Although this is almost the purest form of passive income, it is also one in which your mindset must be about "future" financial freedom. Bonds are slow growing but typically very steady and reliable.

7. Buying Annuities

    Buying annuities can be tricky. As we introduce this source of income, we'll give you tips on what to buy and what to avoid. We'll discuss the pros and cons of buying annuities so that you can decide whether this source of passive income is right for you.

8. Creating Rental Income

    Many people believe this source of passive

income requires $25,000 or more to purchase a rental property, but we'll teach you how to build a rental income with minimal investments of time and money. This is a source that is wide open for innovative thinkers. Rental opportunities are typically growing investments with excellent returns. Notice I didn't say stable? There's no such thing as stable when it comes to passive income. If your source is stable, you're losing money.

9. Buying Mortgages

Think of these as paper exchanges. You can buy others' mortgages or even become a private lender. This source of passive income can be quite profitable and require little time, but you will need to have some financial backing to begin. This may be one that you'll want to start after you've had some success with your other sources.

10. Product Development and Resale

>Anybody can do this, and it can be a lot of fun. We'll show you how the experts have learned to buy low and sell high. You'll learn to recognize the right products, maintain the proper working inventory, and track your success. Keep your eyes and ears open, and you might also invent a whole new product or service that excites consumers enough to follow you and see what spinoffs may occur.

Using several of these sources, and perhaps more that you find particularly interesting will prepare you for incredible success in building a productive stream of passive income. The reason we suggest many sources, and a variety of ways to use those sources, is because the more sources used, the greater chance you have for success. If one source in the stream fails to produce, go to another. If one source does well for you and then slows to a crawl, it will give you time to focus on other things. Rarely does passive income stream steady, so you ride one while you continue to develop another and another.

That's what makes passive income so different from a regular 9-5 job; you're not stuck in one field or industry. Instead, you can explore and expand your thinking; creativity is the name of the game. Your innovations can be richly rewarding. Instead of being frustrated by short-sighted, status quo superiors who cannot appreciate maverick thinkers like you, you'll find great satisfaction in coming up with new sources of passive income and exciting ways to make those sources work for you.

Remember, you are erecting a platform from which to launch your passive income portfolio. The more sources used, the greater the stream of passive income you will create. Hanging in there for long-term profits is key. Beginning small and building is smart. Creating sources of income with a visionary plan will prepare you for the challenges, setbacks, and successes you will experience along the way. The journey can be bumpy and sometimes the mountain of issues you must overcome can seem insurmountable. If creating passive income happened by the snap of your fingers, there would be so many others out there doing it that the competition would kill your efforts.

This is the perfect time to discuss the advantages of embracing that competitive spirit. We're not talking about the kind of competition that creates bitter rivalries that destroy or cripple one's ability to succeed. That kind of competitive spirit serves no one. However, there is a competition that teaches and inspires you to become better, to learn from others mistakes, and to help you decide how you plan to separate yourself from the pack and provide a unique product or service. So, let's examine the benefits of embracing your competition.

Five Main Benefits of Embracing Your Competition

1. Competition can create in you desire to become the best.

> Musicians having to compete for fans have created some of their most artistic work in their attempts to be better than the rest. Inventors become more innovative problem solvers when they have fierce competition. Technological engineers become more insightful to the needs

of the public when their competition comes knocking at their doors. People who desire to become the best often push themselves to peak performance.

2. Make additional discoveries in the competitive journey.

> Because you are studying your competition to become the best, you will learn a great deal of how and why they do things the way they do. You'll also discover what NOT to do, and change the things you don't like into strategies that will help you become successful. Knowing what others are doing will enable you to engage with the consumers in a different way—in a way that makes your offering unique and allows you to stand out from the crowd.

3. Embracing your competition can save you money and time.

> It's so much easier to learn from someone else's mistakes. There have been many times that I have saved myself money and time by learning what my competition was doing well, adopting those strategies, and then improving on them to do an even better job. Embracing and studying my competition taught me how to work smarter and leaner. Since time means money, any time that can be saved in your startup is of significant value.

4. Competition encourages you to be more creative.

> You can get a lot of ideas from your competition and modify them to suit the way you prefer to do

business. Or, you can just study what doesn't work, why consumers need something new and different, and then create that opportunity for them to shop in a broader marketplace.

5. Most of all, competition creates a need for innovative and ongoing change. Someone else will come in and do something that is different and better, then you adopt that strategy and move forward to improve on it and develop something else different and better. It's ongoing—good for consumers and good for business.

To become successful in creating a good stream of passive income you've got to do two things: a) show consumers why they need what you are offering; and, b) explain why you should be the one to provide that particular product or service. Sounds easy—but it requires thought, planning, time, and money.

CHAPTER 2: A PIPELINE OF E-BOOKS, APPS, AND BLOGS

Creating passive income from these three sources can be labor intensive, or they can be a wonderful outlet for your creative genius. Once you have put the upfront work in, the profits are almost 100%. With very little maintenance and no labor-intensive inventory to worry about, you can begin making money in a matter of weeks. Building a pipeline of e-Books, apps, and blogs can help you to bring in immediate passive income, and you can then take some of that profit to invest in other things.

Why Are e-Books a Good Source of Passive Income

Before you turn off to this subject because you think you don't have the talent to write a book, think again. Remember, you don't have to do the actual writing; you can hire that done by a professional writer. These writers can be found in a variety of places online for a very affordable price. Sites like www.eWriterSolutions.com, www.upworks.com, or www.outsource.com are just a few sources where you can find excellent writers. Why belabor the writing, when for under $250 you can have your book done in a matter of weeks?

Creating a pipeline of eBooks can give you so much flexibility in your work. You can live anywhere that has a high-speed internet connection for your computer and beach-front Margarita's for your celebration when the book has been completed. Because e-Books are digital, you don't have to worry about the cost of print, to lease a warehouse to store inventory, or hiring employees to fulfill orders. We'll discuss later how easy it is to get your book into the hands of consumers.

Even though the information you have provided in your book may be available in other locations, you've taken the time and trouble to gather it all in one book, while putting your own unique twist on the topic. Once you begin writing e-Books, you will soon become the recognized expert. Link your e-Books to a regular blog posting and a website, and you have instant marketing avenues.

The other great thing about writing e-Books is that they have a constant demand, especially if you've learned how to maintain their popularity through effective marketing strategies. This example of the amount of passive income that could be generated with e-Books will excite you. Let's say you had ten e-Books in your passive income pipeline. Now let's estimate a conservative shelf-life of twelve months for each book, and we'll set the price at $5 per book. Let's say you had interesting topics and were selling on average of 10 copies per book per day. Your six-month passive income for all ten books would be $18,250 per year.

Okay, now let's pretend you came up with great topics but did not feel comfortable in writing them yourself, so to hire a professional your writing fees would be $200 per book. Ten books at $200 would cost you a total of $2,000. There are also places online to find a designer to create a great cover for your book. Again, it may cost you $200 per book to have it done, so that would be another $2,000 for all ten books. Taking your writing and design expenses from the $18,250 would leave you $14,250. If you choose to market your books on Amazon, it will usually cost you approximately 30% of the price of the book, which in this case would be $5,475, leaving you $8,775.

Keep in mind, the more e-Books you write, the better you market them, and the longer shelf life they have will just increase the passive income you can expect to make. Starting with only one book is fine, and you can let the proceeds you make from that one help you to pay for the next. Starting small is the way to go. However, you cannot stop after you have written just one, you'll need to keep feeding your pipeline, so the income continues.

To discover how to format your e-Books, visit https://kdp.amazon.com/help?topicId=A17W8UM0MMSQX6#format) or go online to Kindle Direct Publishing (KDP) to access the guidelines you'll need to follow to publish on Amazon or Kindle platforms. You can also use a service like Lulu that will take your uploaded e-Book and place it on multiple platforms for you, instead of you going to each site to upload. Of course, there is an additional charge for that, which is usually another percent or two of the price of your book. To use this service, simply go to https://www.lulu.com, set up your account, and upload your book (2).

If you fancy yourself a writer and plan on using this source extensively to earn passive income, you can also start a blog and website to promote your work. And, if you want to do all your own marketing and fulfillment, you'll keep almost 100% of the profits. Of course, it means more time invested, so weigh all the pros and cons of doing so. The beauty of having Amazon handle everything for you is that you won't have to keep accounts, manage payments, handle distribution, refunds, or returns. You should be able to rely on the platforms you use to provide excellent service. They should also have such a huge market, that it makes the job of promoting your books much easier because you will have a broad base of customers. That's why you pay them 30% of your profits.

With all these resources and tools, all you do is come up with exciting and interesting topics. Try to write about topics that are popular, reach a broad customer base, and that aren't already flooding the market. Although that won't even be a concern if your e-Books contain exceptional information and are well written.

Creating an App as Passive Income

Just like the writing process, you don't have to become a professional coder or programmer to create an incredible app. All the development can be done at an affordable price by the experts. Of course, if you want to take the time to learn to code, you can, but this is time spent that could be better used developing more sources of passive income, don't you think? If you are excited about being the idea man or woman and leaving the labor to those who know how to provide you with an incredible product, then let's move forward, shall we?

One of the most frequently asked questions most people have when developing their first app is—how do I know what kind of app to create? Where do I begin? Here are five easy steps to follow that will help you to decide.

1. Consider a skill or talent you have in which you and others believe to be your particular area of expertise. Perhaps it is a past career, a hobby, or a creative outlet in which you excel. If you can think of nothing you have done where you stood out from the crowd, then think of something that is fascinating to you and perhaps

will also be to a wide range of other people.

2. As you consider your area of expertise, think about a specific problem you had when you were first learning to perform this skill or job. For example, let's say you love to garden and have a talent for growing beautiful vegetables—but, this has not always been the case. Let's say it took you a long time to learn about what soil, seasons, temperatures and sunlight requirements were needed for the many vegetables you were interested in cultivating. Through many trials and errors, much research and failed attempts, you finally have a productive vegetable garden that consistently raises bumper crops. You could design a handy app to resolve the initial issues that you experienced, so that consumers would only be a click away in determining what vegetable to

plant where, when.

3. Now that you have thought of what you want your app to about ask yourself how you can create that app to resolve some of the problems you first experienced. How can you help consumers to achieve greater success investing less time and money?

4. Don't rely entirely on yourself when identifying a problem and solution, especially if you are not an expert in your field of interest. Find people who are currently working in your area of interest or enjoying your hobby and ask lots of questions. Then interview experts to see how they suggest these issues could be resolved. Now, you have the makings of an app.

5. If you simply cannot think of anything, identify some of the day-to-day, repetitive tasks people do that could be achieved more efficiently if they could just click for information. Apps typically provide excellent solutions for repetitive tasks that many people do on a daily basis.

Now you need to focus on how you plan to market and sell your app. Like e-Books, you can sell your app over the Internet by using platforms such as www.e-junkie or www.gumroad.com. Or, you can sell your app on a third-party marketplace like Win 8App Store or Mac App Store. The advantages of using Microsoft or Apple is that they have massive search engines and amazing delivery systems in place. The only way anybody makes money is when your app sells, so everybody works hard to make sure your app is a success (3).

Similar to Amazon for your e-Books, Apple takes about a 30% cut to bring your app to the consumer. They have certain guidelines you must go through for approval, and, of course, there are many apps available, so the competition is high. However, many app developers have not done near the homework or have near the expertise to back up the function of their apps, right? All the support and visibility Apple can provide will more than makes up for the 30% charge.

Blogging is a Beautiful Thing—Six Steps to Success

Starting a blog doesn't have to be rocket science, but your first time out of the gate can be intimidating, especially if you're not a computer whiz. The following are six easy steps to practice that will help you create an incredible blog and maximize the potential passive income you can generate.

Step #1: Ask yourself why you want to start a blog.

I hope your only answer to this question isn't just to make money. Although it's an excellent way to create passive income, if money is your only reason, you're setting yourself up for failure. Blogs that are started because someone wants to make a difference, to become a better person, or to get published, are going to be ones that attract a bigger following. Unless you are blogging about ways to increase your income—like generating passive income—talking about income made from your blog won't be terribly impressive.

Step #2: What will be the focus of your blog?

What are your hobbies, talents, and things in which

you are passionate? When you're with a group of people, what do you find yourself talking about most of the time? That may be your first blog. Make sure the topic of your blog is broad enough to continue sharing information about it over an extended period.

Step #3: What blogging platforms do you plan to use?

There are many free hosting sites; however, since your blog is to promote whatever will create passive income for you, it is better to have a self-hosted WordPress blog. Besides, free blog sites aren't ever free because the myriad of limitations they place on you will inhibit your ability to reach maximum followers. What are the costs of a self-hosted blog? With many hosting accounts, you can get a domain name for free. The average fee for an account is approximate $75 for the first year.

Web Hosting Hub is reliable and affordable. They provide excellent customer support with 99.9% server uptime. They offer a free domain name, and their service is quite easy for beginners. They also offer unlimited bandwidth, disk space, and email accounts. If you are not satisfied, Web Hosting Hub offers a 90-day money back guarantee. If you decide blogging is not for you, you can simply cancel your account and ask for a refund.

Step #5: Create Your Blog

Since this is dependent on which host you chooses to use, the best thing to do is search online for the web host you desire and follow their step-by-step guidelines.

Step #6: Start Blogging

If you have chosen a reputable web host, it is as simple as logging in with your username and password and posting your first blog. Decide how often you wish to post a new blog, and let your readers know. Also, link your blog to your website and your e-Books. This will create excellent synergy for the promotion of all your sources of passive income. The best blogs are ones that are fun, informative, fun, creative, fun, theme based—oh, and did I mention fun (4)?

Whichever sources you decide to use, or if you incorporate all of them into your passive income portfolio, make it entertaining for your followers and yourself. If building passive income becomes a chore, you're not going to want to give up your free time and spare money to make it work. So, the best advice that I can give you is to choose sources of passive income that you will enjoy, and you think others will as well.

CHAPTER 3: REAL ESTATE RETURNS

Owning real estate rental property is a long-term investment. Although it is not as liquid as cash in hand or the bank, it can eventually net you quite a return, especially if you have positive cash flow from your rental. There are certain things to keep in mind when investing in rental property, and they are as follows:

10 Tips for Investing in Rental Property

1. The location is everything.

Make sure your location will support the rent amount needed to cover your mortgage. If not, you'll end up with a negative cash flow that will eat into your passive income. No matter how well-maintained the home or apartment building you are purchasing is, it's not going to be consistently rented if the surrounding neighborhood is dangerous or poorly kept—unless, of course, you plan on being a slum lord, and that's a whole other headache.

2. When investing, don't be shy about asking for the moon in your purchase contract.

The worse that could happen is that the owner will refuse your offer, and then you can counter in hopes of finding the best possible price. Before you begin the negotiations, decide on what your ceiling offer is, and stick to that figure. The price you pay for the property should be well below the appraised value so that you can start as a landlord in an equal position.

Include, in writing, any additional appliances, fans, and window coverings you want to go with the sale. Also, be aware of other costs that will need to be paid upfront, such as HOA transfer fees and appraisal fees. Because these fees must be paid before the property closes, you don't want to get stuck with these out-of-pocket costs should the property not close. A good practice in these situations is to negotiate that the owner pays these costs and closing costs if possible. If the owner insists on splitting these fees, then negotiate that the owner pays up front and be reimbursed as closing. That way, if the property doesn't close, you won't be out the money.

Since you want to invest as little upfront money as

possible, negotiate everything that you can to be put into the mortgage. For example, raise the price of the property and have the owner pay for the closing costs; this will enable you to purchase with no upfront closing costs. Your closing costs will be wrapped into your mortgage. Look for properties that have been on the market for some time, since the owners will be more open to negotiating price or perks. NEVER, EVER purchase property without doing a thorough inspection by a paid professional. When repairs need to be made, either has the repairs completed before closing or ask that the owners renegotiate their asking price.

If the property already has a tenant, realize that you will most likely need to give them a 30-day notice or honor the existing lease agreement. Ask the owners to review the existing rental agreement to see what your obligations are regarding the current tenant.

Make sure you have also done an excellent job considering what rents are going for in that area, and see how those properties compare with the one you are interested in purchasing.

3. The best investment isn't always the prettiest property.

Keep in mind; this is to be a rental property—not one in which you are planning to live. Any improvements made should be practical and economical, not necessarily the most expensive and luxurious. It is usually not a good idea to have a lot of extras on a rental, like a pool or a fireplace, for instance. They create additional liabilities, and the cost of maintenance or upkeep cannot be recouped in rental fees.

4. Be prepared for repairs after each vacating tenant.

Tenants are going to damage your property, and you need to be prepared, so you are not blindsided by costly repairs. It's important that you require regular inspections of the property, done by yourself or your management company. If you see that the property is neglected or abused, give your immediate tenant notice to vacate before you lose money and valuable time making unnecessary repairs. Even though having a management company will cost you a little money upfront, they can save you so much in the long run. Not only will they save you money, but if you actually want passive income from your rentals, then you need to distance yourself from the day-to-day hassles of rental management.

5. Increase rental incomes for long-term tenants.

The mistake many investors make is that they fail to

raise rents for long-term tenants. Your leases should have potential built-in rate increases that are written into the lease agreements. If you have an excellent tenant, then you'll want to reward them by maintaining a reasonable rental fee. However, that doesn't mean raising the rent. If your tenant has been in the property for a long time, you will still be expected to paint and replace flooring from time to time, and your rental fees will need to cover those costs. Set aside enough positive cash flow to cover repairs and updates to your rental. This will keep it market fresh and make it more appealing to a wide range of potential tenants.

6. Plan on regular tax increases and elevated HOA fees.

Before purchasing your property review what the taxes and HOA fees have done over the past five years. Were the taxes steady, or have they increased substantially? Look at the amount they have increased over this period, and plan on that continuing. The same can be said for HOA fees. First of all, make sure you have included HOA fees in your rental fees because you will be responsible for paying them—not the tenant. You don't want to have taxes and HOA fees eat up your passive income from the property, so those costs should be figured into your rentals.

7. Keep as much money in your pocket as possible.

There are many ways to purchase property that won't cost you an arm and a leg for a down payment and closing costs. In fact, you can buy cooperatively with other investors for as little as $5,000, and enjoy all the benefits of passive income in your rental. If you decide on this method of investing in real estate, make sure you have spelled out in your agreement the requirements of selling your portion of the property. The downside to these types of investments is that it can often be harder to sell your ownership share.

If you decided that shared real estate investment is a way for you to get your foot in the door, one such company to check into is RealtyShares. RealtyShares is one of the largest real estate crowdsourcing companies, and it is based in San Francisco. They include a variety of nationwide investment opportunities in both residential and commercial properties. This can be quite advantageous as you can pick and choose locations around the country, purchasing when the markets are at their best (5).

8. Don't outstay your welcome in a rental investment.

What I mean by that is that every property has a predetermined useful life. Don't keep the property beyond its earning potential. If the repairs you are consistently making outweigh the return, it may be time to sell and reinvest in another rental. Track your appreciation to determine whether your money would earn you more in a different area of property. In most markets and locations, the life of a property is, at its maximum, no longer than 29 years. The life of a property is dependent upon its age at purchase, and whether it is residential or commercial. Some commercial property has a longer life than residential.

9. You can also trade properties of like type and value.

There are tax requirements to consider when trading properties, and a professional can help you with this. However, this can be an excellent way to gain instant equity in a property, since the trade does not have term requirements, but only refers to the purchase price. For example, if you have a property that has no equity but is in a great location, and you want cash to invest in additional passive income opportunities, you could trade with someone who does have equity. After the trade, you could then pull some of the equity from your newly acquired property to invest in several others without any out-of-pocket costs.

10. You can also purchase paper (privately held notes or deeds) on a property.

This usually requires more money, but there is no maintenance or upkeep—you are only purchasing the paper. You don't own the property, unless, of course, the payee should default—which would mean you own the entire property for a fraction of the price. When you purchase paper, you own the paper or the loan.

For example, let's say the original owner sold the home that he owned free and clear and created a private mortgage or loan on the property for the buyers. Each month, the buyer makes a payment of $1,000 to the original owner. Because the original owner was willing to carry the financing, he receives significantly more interest on his money—let's say 10%. The remainder owed on loan is $50,000 at 10% interest.

For personal reasons, the original owner decides he needs cash and wants to sell the private note he is carrying at a substantial discount. It is feasible that you could purchase a $50,000 note for $30,000 and make 10% interest on your investment. You will still have to honor the terms of the original loan, but you have just made $20,000, and you will earn a good deal more money on your investment. Of course, you too have the option to sell the paper to another investor like yourself who is also interested in purchasing the paper.

Don't worry about the chances of the buyers defaulting because that is not a bad thing for your investment. If they default, then you are the owner of the property. The more equity in the property, the better. In fact, a good rule of thumb when investing in the paper is that there should be at least 10% equity in the property. More equity is always better, but 10% equity is a must.

There are so many different opportunities to make passive income in real estate investments; whatever you can imagine can usually be created in a purchase agreement. Just be careful that you have done your homework and that you are not buying something with an inflated price or unreasonable terms. If you find that real estate is your primary source of passive income, you may want to consider obtaining a real estate license so you can save yourself the commissions on the property you sell and get paid the commissions on ones you purchase. That's a whole other source of passive income. It doesn't require any more work than your original purchase, and you'll be putting commissions in your pocket.

CHAPTER 4: INVESTING IN STOCKS, BONDS & ANNUITIES

Investing in stocks, bonds, and annuities can mean a chunk of change, so you may want to start out smaller and work your way up to this type of passive income. Let your money work for you on your other ventures and then use those profits to invest in stocks, bonds, and annuities. You can also make interest off CDs held in the bank, but today's rates are so low it won't gain you much income. There are different ways to invest in stocks, but if you are unfamiliar with the market the best way is to hire a reputable broker.

The safest way to invest your money is to do so with

stable, reliable companies. Your returns won't be huge, but, as I said before, passive income is not a get-rich-quick scheme. You've got time, so it's probably better to play it safe and let your passive income gradually build. Of course, you're not always going to come out a winner, so if you're the anxious type who watches his or her money fluctuate each day and gets stressed with the roller-coaster ride of trading stocks, then this is not the best option for you.

If you decide to give it a try, develop a relationship with a good broker. Communicate your goals to your broker and trust them to help you choose which stocks to invest in and what is better left to the high-risk players. There are also stock options you can consider, but those are beyond the scope of this book. It will take some research for you to decide which stock to purchase and how many shares. If you are interested, the best thing is to research, study the market for a while before investing, and then pick a few favorites to watch for a while before you lay down the cash.

Diversify your stocks so that if one is down perhaps the others will be on the rise. Don't invest more than you can afford to lose. Investing in dividend-bearing stocks is an excellent way to draw money on your investment without selling the stock periodically. Choosing stable, reliable companies will enable you to collect regularly paid dividends and still leave your investment and let it continue to create more passive income. By choosing well, diversifying your portfolio, and investing several thousand dollars in dividend-based stock, you stand to make four to five percent on your investment without selling. It's passive but, don't kid yourself; it can be quite stressful.

If you're planning the DIY type of stock investing, let

us warn you that the learning curve can be very expensive. Years ago, a close friend of my family decided to spend her $35,000 inheritance in the stock market. She thought it would be fun to become a day trader and work from home, and felt her inheritance would give her a good start. She read up and studied the market for months before finally quitting her job and buying her stock. Within a matter of six months, she had lost all her money and was out looking for another job. Although day trading can sound like a lot of fun, it requires knowledge and nerves of steel to hang in there through the ups and downs of the market.

One of the best investments for a novice trader is Exchange-Traded Funds (ETFs). These are investments that have assets such as stocks, bonds, and commodities; however, they are easier to understand and much more liquid. They also come with a lower price tag than investing in mutual funds. ETFs are especially rewarding for the young investor who doesn't have much money to spend so he or she would be unable to make a broker's deposit of $5,000 to $10,000, but they would enjoy a higher-risk stock. ETFs could either be included in their portfolio, or the trader could invest in ETFs entirely. It is still required, however, to pay a broker's fee on every ETF transaction (6).

Investing in Bonds and Bank Savings

These are probably the safest investment, and yet your gains will be minimal. If you have waited until you are retired to begin building passive income, these are not going to mature quickly enough to make a difference. They are such a solid investment, and you can count on them to grow to match inflation, but not much more. The biggest risk made when investing in bonds is that you have left money on the table by not putting your money somewhere else that could have grown faster and significantly increased your passive income.

There are short-term and long-term bonds with differing maturity dates. Think of bonds like a loan and the maturity date as the time in which the bond issuer is required to pay you back the entire loan amount. The longer the term to maturity, the more time you'll have to collect interest on the bond. The benefit to you for lending the money is that you get to collect interest on the bond, and at the time of maturity, you get back your initial investment. The only time you would not get your investment back is if the issuer has defaulted or you sell the bond to another investor before its maturity.

If you want to avoid broker fees, you can purchase

bonds directly from the Treasure. Just visit their online site at http://www.treasurydirect.gov, and everything will be handled electronically. If you are using a broker and have decided to include bonds in your portfolio, you will then pay a broker's fee. Most brokers will ask for a minimum deposit of $5,000 to $10,000 to open your account and invest your money, so be prepared (7).

Bank CDs are less of a risk than bonds, but they also provide fewer returns. The beauty of CDs is that they are liquid (easily converted to cash) should you need your money in a hurry. The problem with CDs in today's market is their interest is so low; your money is better spent in another passive source. The interest on a CD depends on how much you put into the CD and how long you plan to leave it there. You can put thousands into a CD and commit to leaving it there for years and still get no more than 1 or 2 percent return.

No risk—no return. It would probably cost you more in gas to pick up your money.

Investing in Annuities

Annuities are typically purchased from an insurance company. You buy the policy and then it pays you a specified amount each year for the rest of your life. The younger you are when you invest in the annuity, the less it will pay you each year. The dangers with annuities are that the insurance company might go belly-up and leave you holding the bag. For this reason, choose insurance companies that have been around for years and have proven themselves in the marketplace. You also may wish to diversify when investing in annuities, spreading your money with several insurance companies.

Annuities can also be inherited, but make sure you communicate to your beneficiary any annuity you may have. Insurance companies are not held liable to inform recipients that their deceased donor had an annuity that was willed to them and they are now the recipient of thousands of dollars. Don't hold your breath on that happening! If your chosen beneficiary doesn't know to call and notify the insurance company of the change in name or status of the annuity, they might not ever collect. By the time your intended beneficiary got around to discovering you willed your annuity to them, the insurance company may well have eaten up the profits in service fees (8).

If you are a bit intimidated with the thought of investing in stocks and annuities, that's understandable. Starting small is difficult with these types of investments, especially if your broker requires large deposits. Some brokerage houses will allow novice investors to begin with minimum deposits of a few thousand dollars, and some offer you investment money to sign up with their investment firm. A word of caution, be careful when going with brokers who entice with free offers. There might be a good reason they feel as though they must pay for their clients.

Investing in the market is not for the faint of heart. So, if you don't do stress—don't invest, especially if you are investing money that you would lose sleep over if you lost it tomorrow. Stick to other ways to create passive income that won't give you heartburn if you should drop a few thousand during your learning curve. For some, that could be all the money they have saved or earned by their entire stream of passive income. Don't risk it all—instead, start small!

CHAPTER 5: BUILDING/BUYING WEBSITES & DOMAINS

There is a whole new world of online commerce out there in the form of websites and domains. You can build them, buy them, or flip them, but whatever you do will mean some upfront investment of time and money. Of course, you can always think of a domain name, register it, and use or sell it. You can do the same with a website—build it or pay for it to be built, then use it to promote your stream of passive income. Sounds good, but those of you who have ever attempted to have experts create a website for you know the expense and frustration that can cause. The DIY job of building a website doesn't get you the optimization you'll need to put your business on the map. So, what do you do?

The first website I built was through GoDaddy. While it looked good, it was not successful at driving browsers to my site. I knew nothing of keywords, WordPress, reviews, ads, links, nothing—and so that is what the website was worth to my business—absolutely nothing. Then I met with an SEO and paid to have the website optimized. Eight-hundred dollars later, I still had an attractive website, and I believed the SEO was working on my behalf to make the site more functional, but, to tell you the truth, after months of asking where we were at with the optimization, I still had a whole lot of nothing. No more responses, very little traffic, and an empty purse.

Next, I hired a professional design company to give me a fresh start and create a whole new website for my business. This time I paid $16,000, and it looked outstanding. It was highly functioning, did exactly what I wanted it to do, drove business to the site, but there was one problem. I could not maintain the site myself. About once a week I had a challenge on the site that needed attention, and there I was— dependent upon the web designers to change the code and make the site work more efficiently. So now, not only was it highly expensive, it was extremely time-consuming. I ended up selling the business after 18 months. It was profitable, and the woman who purchased my business also owns the website. It was still a startup with existing contracts of over $60,000. The company sold for $32,000, which was barely enough to cover my cost of developing and maintaining the website during those miserable 18 months.

Who reaped the benefits of my website business? The person who purchased it; she didn't have to go through the months of frustrating design and content development or the initial start-up hassles for website maintenance and support. Since this was years ago, I didn't know about website sales, and they might not have even existed back then. I didn't sell my site; I sold my business. The problem was, I didn't think of my website as my business; I thought of it as a way to market my business.

The reason I share this story is that I wanted to give you a better perspective on how to think of a website. When I refer to selling websites, what I'm talking about is selling businesses. There are many sites online that have listings of website businesses for sale. They range from $50 on up to $15,000 or more. Sometimes the better bargain is not to build your site from scratch, but to buy a bargain business and let it provide immediate passive income.

There will always be the high-priced website companies that you pass by because you think they are cost prohibitive, but stop for a moment and give it a second look. If it is already making a sizeable passive income, you may want to take on a partner and do a little coop investing. Then there are the budget website businesses that you, again, pass by because you believe they couldn't be worth the hosting fees, right? Not necessarily. Look again. If the website is of interest to you, examine it to see how you could ramp up the site and generate new business. If all you save is the cost of website design, that, in itself, could mean thousands of dollars in your pocket.

Then there are the website businesses that are not too flashy, but they consistently perform. For most of you first-time website buyers, this will be the place to start to build up your site passive income (9). If your talent lies in writing code or programming, what are you thinking? Start building businesses around a website and then sell it, for goodness sake! Or, partner with a content writer, and together create some unusual sources for making passive income.

A real inexpensive way to build passive income is by buying domain names. They are inexpensive and, if you've done your homework, can be sold for incredible profits. Let me give you five easy to remember tips on what not to do when you're planning to buy and sell domain names.

5 Easy Tips on What Not to Do When Buying Domains

1. Don't cruise lots of sites looking for domain names, or versions of the domain names you like, to see if they are taken. Decide where you want to purchase your domain, and stick to that sight. Most domain names cost $10. If you find the domain is available, buy it immediately. Don't wait until after dinner because, if it's a hot name that just happened to become available, it will be taken by then.

2. Don't ask other people what they think of your domain name. It might give them the idea to buy it from you and then sell back to you for a profit.

3. Don't buy just one version of the same domain. They are only $10, buy up the .net, .com, .org, .biz, all of them. What do you think another who likes your name will do when they see the domain is taken and not for sale? They will usually go to another version of the same name. For example, if .com is taken, they'll choose .net. If you own all the versions of the same domain, you can sell the .com version to them for a sizeable profit.

4. Don't buy a lot of domain names that you just think are cool. Look to see what the latest trends are in business. New business start-ups are public record, and corporations must publish their openings in the paper. Search to find what types of businesses are popular and then put yourself in the place of the owner. What names might relate to those kinds of

businesses? Then, simply buy the domains.

5. Don't feel like you can't ask for a lot of money because you only paid $10 for the domain. Many rookie business owners fail to set up their businesses correctly, and that includes registering their names. By the time they get around to doing so, their preferred name is taken, and they are then required to pay much, much more for the domain name. You were the visionary, and you should reap the benefits.

Finding places to buy and sell websites and domains are just a matter of a little online research. Many sites will lead you to these wonderful little gold mines of passive income.

CHAPTER 6: MONITOR & ADJUST YOUR SOURCES

Even though all these sources for passive income eventually take very little time, you still need to monitor the results of your investments and make the necessary adjustments for them to continue to run smoothly. If you're writing eBooks and creating apps, you need to keep your pipeline filled with current books and apps continually. If you are purchasing a rental property, you'll need to continuously search the market for bargains and determine which of your current assets are ready to be sold. If you are buying and selling websites and domains, it's a constant search for good little businesses and names. Think of yourself as the CEO of your passive income business. You don't have to do the grunt labor, just show up now and then.

Now you know why I said in the very beginning that it takes a lot of creativity and innovative thinking to create viable passive income. Don't turn this endeavor into a job, keep it adventurous. This is your chance to be an entrepreneur, to discover all the many ways or different businesses you can create that take little to no startup cost with a minimal amount of time spent in maintaining their ongoing profits.

I will tell you; it will be quite tempting to spend your passive income when you see it begin to roll in but resist. Celebrate just a little, briefly indulge yourself, then set aside some money for more investments and always save. I've found that when you have passive income and things get tough, everything comes crashing down at once. It can be very discouraging, and many who made a good start on building passive income quit during the first storm because they weren't prepared to ride it out—both financially and emotionally.

By monitoring and adjusting what works and what

doesn't work, your stream will stay active and your passive income consistent. Frequently examine the cost, in time and money, to maintain your sources of passive income. If one source of passive income costs you more time than you want to devote to it, drop it. That's not failing; it's called smart business practices. Some sources you don't have to drop; just let them ride away into the sunset until they dry up and stop producing altogether. However, there are other things you will need to shut down, or the small strings of business will make you crazy to maintain them. It will be too much work for too little returns.

Always search for new sources of passive income. What you think are great sources today will become obsolete tomorrow. It's an ever-changing ocean of newness; to be most successful you must surf the curl or be buried by the waves of change. Stay current with technology, and learn how to make it work for you. Technology an excellent tool, even if used only to track your successes and setbacks. Make technology your business partner; in doing so, you can often create new business in a matter of days and change existing ones at the click of a key.

This doesn't have to be a business of one. In some of my businesses, I've taken on partners who were more technically savvy than me, or who were experts in the field in which I wished to learn more. That doesn't mean you should partner in every source of your passive income, but in some avenues having a partner enables you to make more money in less time. If you do take on a partner, make sure you have clearly communicated your expectations and put everything in writing.

Most importantly, and I cannot emphasize this

enough, make it FUN! Build passive income by doing the things you've always wanted to do, by creating unique and entertaining profitable avenues of revenue. It is so much easier to market businesses that you believe in and enjoys. It's just natural to want to talk to your friends about what you're doing when you love your work.

I've heard it said that work should fund your life but not be your life. I'm not so sure this is the case with passive income. What you enjoy most in life soon becomes the work that you enjoy most. I love my work so much; it's difficult for me to separate the two at times. I can't imagine going on vacation and not thinking about what my sources of passive income are doing while I'm away. Most people think of their pets having a field day while they are away, but those of us who love creating passive income have better things on which to focus. We know the importance of keeping our creative juices flowing all the time. Think of your passive income as a game—a game where you get to make the rules and determine the outcomes.

Be prepared for some ups and downs, especially when you first begin building your stream. If you're going to ride the rapids, you'll have to learn to navigate the rocky patches without drowning. It's an important time to share with a loved one or close friend what you are planning to do—someone who will encourage you—someone, with whom you can celebrate your successes. Choose these people carefully because, in the beginning, stage of your new passive income career, they may be the determining factor of whether you hang in there or drop out. Good luck with your efforts. Keep me posted; I'll love to share in all your victories.

THANK YOU

Dear treasured reader, I would like to thank you from the bottom of my heart for choosing to purchase this book. I hope you've gotten some valuable information that you can use right now to build a successful online business for yourself. If you liked it, would you be so kind as to leave an honest/positive review for my book on amazon. I would appreciate it very much.

In case you missed it earlier, if you would like to receive latest tips and tricks on internet marketing, exclusive strategies, upcoming books & promotions, and **more,** do subscribe to my mailing list in the link below! I will be giving away a free book that you can download *right away* as well after you subscribe to show my appreciation!

Here's the link: http://bit.do/jonathanswalker

Additionally if you want to build other kinds of online business' you can check out my other books here at: www.amazon.com/author/jonathanswalker

Once again thank you and all the best to your success!

Jonathan S. Walker

About The Author

Hi there it's Jonathan Walker here, I want to share a little bit about myself so that we can get to know each other on a deeper level. I grew up in California, USA, and have lived there for the better part of my life. Being exposed to many different people and opportunities when I was young, it made me want to strive to become an entrepreneur to escape the rat race path that most of my peers had taken. I knew I wanted to be able to travel and experience the world the way it was meant to be seen and I've done just that. I've travelled to most places around the world and I'm enjoying every minute of it for sure. In my free time I love to play tennis and believe it or not, compose songs. I wish you all the best again in your endeavours, and may your dreams, whatever they may be, come true abundantly in the near future.

CPSIA information can be obtained
at www.ICGtesting.com
Printed in the USA
LVHW012306241020
669607LV00005B/458